D1060734

Go, FedEx!

WRITTEN BY BROOKE PARKER JUSTICE
ILLUSTRATED BY MALLORY LIGHTMAN LESTER

Brooke's Books

FedEx service marks used by permission

International Standard Book Number (ISBN)
978-0-692-52494-7

Printed in the United States of America

For my parents -
Thank you for instilling in me the confidence to do what makes me happy no matter what.
Dad, I am so proud of all you have accomplished in your 37 years at FedEx. This is for you!
—Brooke Parker Justice

For my nephews Colin and Griffin,
"There is nothing more truly artistic than to love people."
— Vincent Van Gogh
Always stay inspired.
—Mallory Lightman Lester

Don't you love to see
those FedEx planes
flying way up in the sky?
Have you ever noticed
they don't have windows
and asked yourself, "Well, why?"

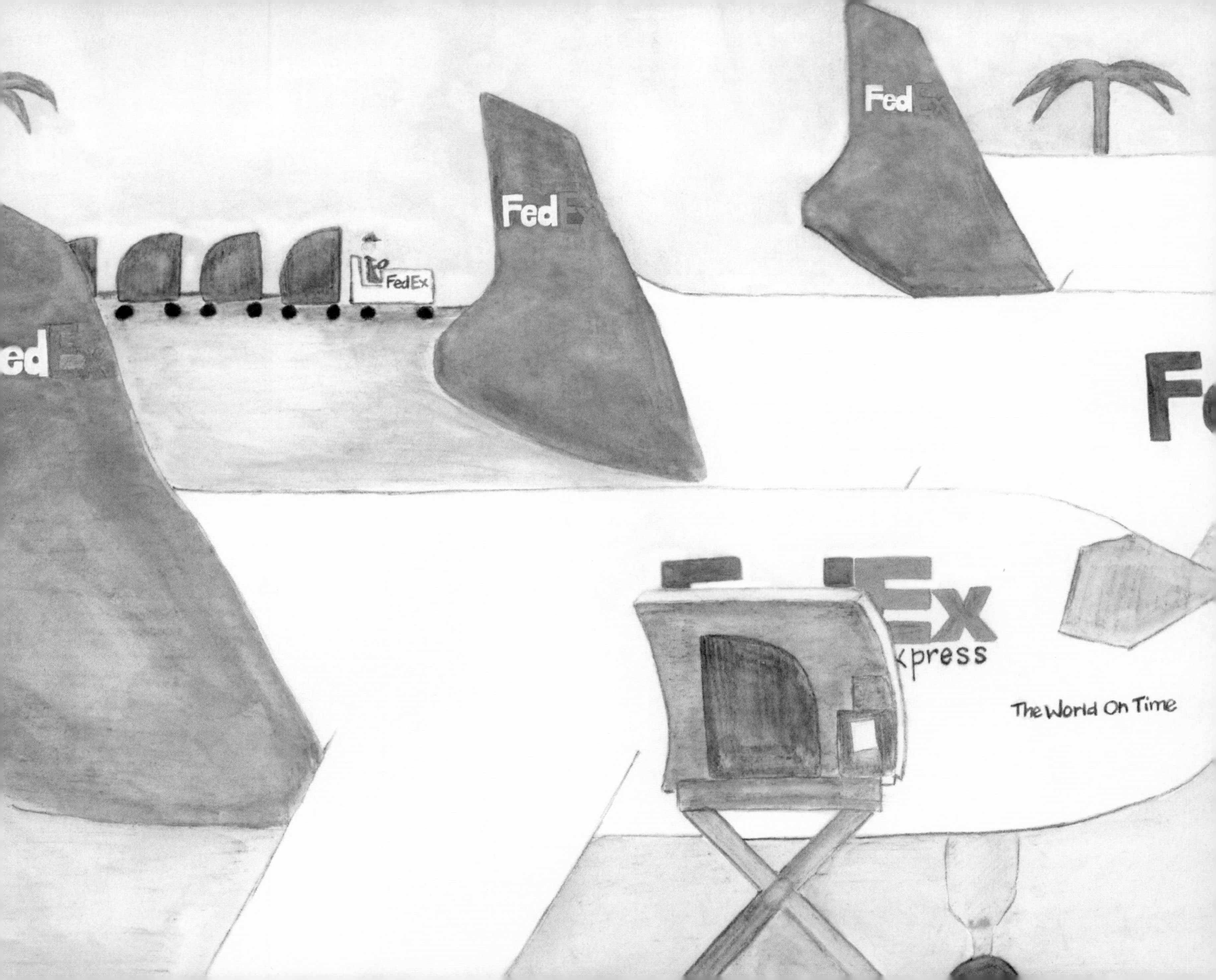
FedEx
FedEx
FedEx
The World On Time

FedEx planes are different
from the ones that carry you and me.
Their planes carry packages
everywhere – even across the sea!
(And it all started
in Memphis, Tennessee.)

FedEx
FedEx
FedEx
FedEx
BEALE
BB
KING'S
Schwab
CHARLES VERGOS
Rendezvous
CHARCOAL RIBS
LOOK GOOD
Beauty Shop
EAT GOOD
CAFE
OLÉ
YOUNG
COOPER
DELI
BEALE STREET FLIPPERS
BEALE STREET FLIPPERS

A man named Fred Smith
had a bright idea to
send packages overnight.
He wondered how to do it
and thought,
"Aha! The fastest way is flight!"

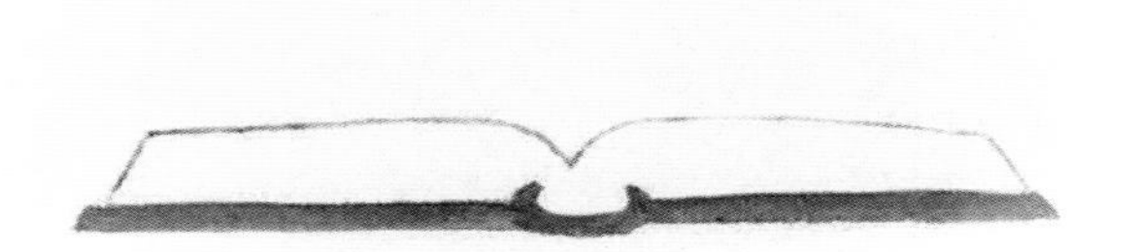

YALE
FRED SMITH

He was smart and hatched a plan
to make it happen.
He said, "First, I'll need some planes,
and then I'll need some captains."

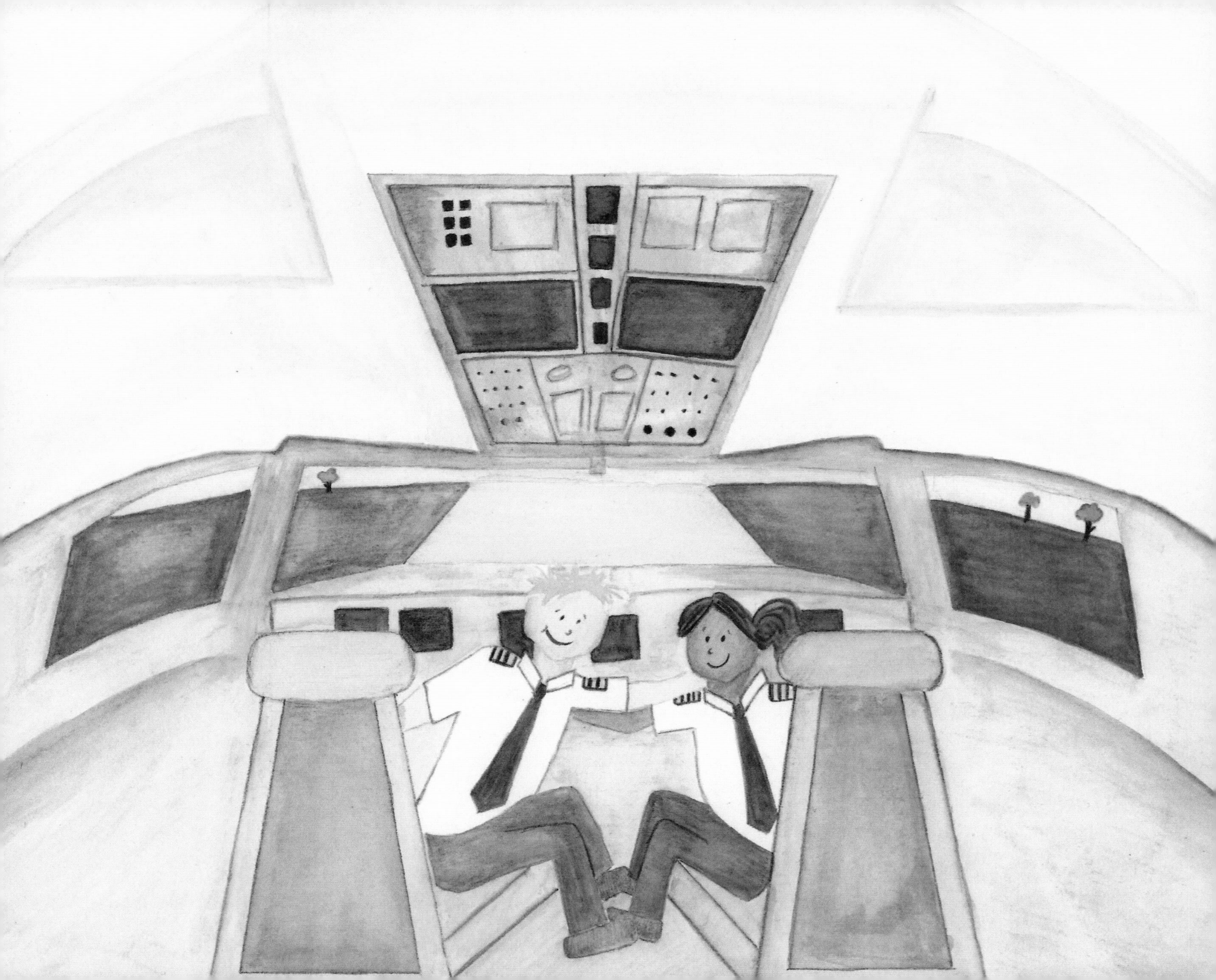

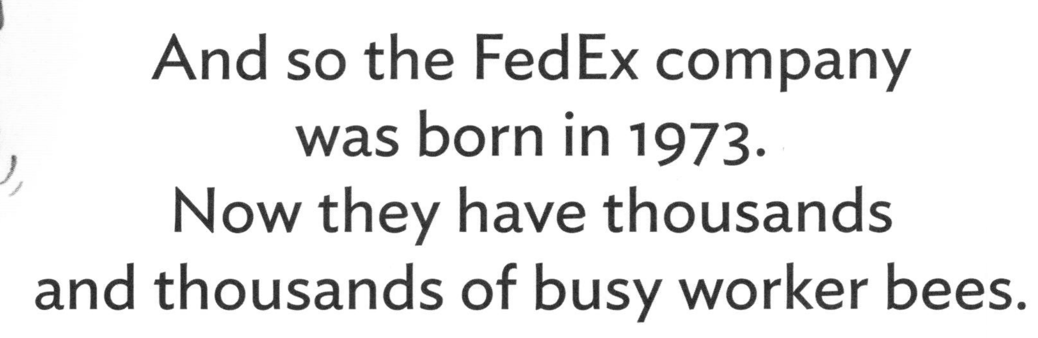

And so the FedEx company
was born in 1973.
Now they have thousands
and thousands of busy worker bees.

FedEx
FedEx
FRAGILE
BEE
CAREFUL

A plane is not the only way
their packages can travel.
They can also go by truck
or train and some
are marked as “fragile.”

FedEx
FedEx
FedEx
FedEx
Freight
FedEx
FedEx

Packages come in and out
of a special place called the hub.
The hub is where the packages
are sorted – they've even shipped
giant panda cubs!

FedEx
FedEx
FedEx
LIVE ANIMAL
FedEx
FedEx
FedEx

The hub is a very exciting place to be.
You can hear the roaring of the jets
and the workers shouting, “Yippee!”

FedEx
FedEx
FedEx
FedEx
FRAGILE
DELIVER TO TROOPS
800-4-FLOWER
I ♥ U MOM
FedEx
FRAGILE
FedEx
FedEx

The people of FedEx
work all day and night
to make sure that your package
is delivered just right.

FedEx
FedEx
FedEx
FedEx
FedEx
FedEx
FedEx

So at the end of a long day,
when you are snuggled in your bed,
FedEx is flying from here to there
right above your head!

FedEx
FedEx

Brooke is a teacher, wife to Will, mother to Carlyle, and daughter to Diane and Jim Parker. She earned her bachelor's degree from the University of Alabama and later her Master of Arts in Teaching with a focus in elementary education from Belmont University. Her father has worked at FedEx for the past 37 years, and his career there (and love for all things FedEx) inspired Brooke to write a book about the company she has grown up with in the great city of Memphis, Tennessee. As an elementary school teacher, she wanted to write down the story of FedEx in words that children could understand. She hopes you have as much fun reading this book as she did writing it!

A life-long artist and proud Memphian, Mallory has a passion for life, love and live music. She earned her Bachelor of Arts degree, concentrating in Graphic Design, with an Advertising minor from The University of Alabama. After returning home from college, she fell in love with her husband, Stephen, and they have enthusiastically added two dogs (Archie and Teddy) and two cats (Elphie and Oz) to their family. She practiced graphic design at her family's business for seven happy years and now runs her graphic design online Etsy store, Mallory's Galleries.
She is thrilled to get to work with Brooke, a long-time friend, on this wonderful, creative project!